AIM Higher!
Reading Comprehension
Level D

Standardized
Assessment:
Strategies for
Success

Level D

Shepherd • Salinger • Castro
Stevenson • Choi

aim higher!
Great Source Education Group
A Houghton Mifflin Company
Wilmington, MA

Staff Credits

Editorial

Diane Perkins Castro

Annie Sun Choi

Sharon S. Salinger

Robert D. Shepherd

Kelsey Stevenson

Production & Design

Paige Larkin

Matthew Pasquerella

First Edition

Printed in the United States of America

3 4 5 6 7 8 9 10   CRW   05 04 03 02 01

International Standard Book Number: 1-58171-057-7

CONTENTS

INTRODUCTION

Knowing how to read well is very important. That is why every school wants its students to learn this skill. Schools give reading tests to find out how well their students can read. This book will help you practice for such tests. It will also help you to understand better what you read. Then reading will be easier and more enjoyable.

There are ten reading selections in this book. Some of the selections present information. Some tell stories, true or made-up. One is a poem. Following each selection, there are ten multiple-choice questions. You will read each selection and answer the questions about it. You may look back at the reading selections at any time to find the answers.

The first selection is from the book *The Tarantula in My Purse and 172 Other Wild Pets*. After you read the selection, you should answer the questions that follow it. Next, you will study six lessons. These lessons explain each kind of question found on reading tests. Each lesson shows you how to find the right answer for questions about the selection.

After you study the lessons and learn how to answer questions, it will be time to move on to Selection 2. For this selection, the book will tell you what kinds of question you are answering. If you need help, you can go back to the lesson that teaches you how to answer that kind of question.

The rest of the selections and questions look just as they would on a real reading test. Read these stories and answer the questions to practice what you have learned. Then you will be ready to take reading tests.

Cross-Curricular Icons Used in this Book

Note to the teacher: Reading comprehension is a skill that is directly addressed in English classes but is applicable to every curricular area. The selections in this book cover a broad range of topics in various curricular areas. The authors and editors of this book have used the following icons throughout to identify the curricular areas treated in the selections:

 The Arts

 Geography and Global Studies

 History and Social Science

 Language and Literature

 Mathematics

 Science and Technology

DIRECTIONS

Read this story about a girl and her special pet. Then answer questions 1 through 10.

The Screech Owl Who Liked Television
by Jean Craighead George

[Editor's note: The author, or writer, of this true story is an animal lover. She and her family like to care for wild animals who need help. Twig is the writer's little girl.]

Twig's favorite pet was a small gray screech owl. Had he not fallen from his nest before he could fly, he would have lived in the open woodland, deciduous forest,[1] park, town, or river's edge. But he had landed on a hard driveway instead and ended up in our house. He was round-eyed and hungry. He looked up at Twig and gave the quivering hunger call of the screech owl. Twig named him Yammer.[2]

Yammer quickly endeared himself to us. He hopped from his perch to our hands to eat. He rode around the house on our shoulders and sat on the back of a dining-room chair during dinner.

Before the green of June burst upon us, Yammer had become a person to Twig, who felt all wild friends were humans and should be treated as such.

Wild animals are not people. But Twig was not convinced. One Saturday morning she and Yammer were watching a cowboy show on television. They had been there for hours.

---

1 **deciduous forest.** Woods with trees that lose their leaves
2 **Yammer.** *To yammer* means to complain or talk a lot

"Twig," I said, "you've watched TV long enough. Please go find a book to read, or do your homework." My voice was firm. I kept the TV in my bedroom just so the children wouldn't be constantly tempted to turn it on as they had when it was downstairs.

Reluctantly, Twig got to her feet. At the door she turned and looked at her little owl. He was on top of the headboard, staring at the screen. A rider on a horse was streaking across the desert. From an owl's point of view, the pair were mouse-sized.

"How come Yammer can watch TV and I can't?" she asked, pouting.

Hardly had she spoken than Yammer pushed off from the headboard, struck the prey with his talons,[3] and dropped to the floor, bewildered.

Twig rushed to his rescue. She gathered him up and hugged him to her chest. With a scornful glance at me, she hurried to her room. The small owl's round yellow eyes were peering from between her gently curled fingers.

Twig was right: This otherworldly creature[4] was a person. Wasn't his menu of mice and crickets included on the shopping list? Didn't he have his own bedroom in the gap between the Roger Tory Peterson field guides[5] in the living-room bookcase? Didn't he run down into the cozy blanket-tunnels made by Twig at bedtime and utter his note of contentment? And didn't he like TV just as she did?

Most scientists are taught not to read human emotions into animals, but sometimes they wonder about the truth of it. When you live with animals, they often seem quite humanlike.

Later that morning of the TV incident, I looked in on Twig and Yammer. The owl was perched on the top of her open door, preening his feathers.[6] She was sitting with her chin in her hands, looking at him.

"I feel sorry for Yammer," she said. "He's stuck in this house. He needs to see things that move like they do in the woods."

"So?" I said.

"So, I've finished my homework and made my bed. Can Yammer and I watch TV?"

I heard myself whisper, "Yes." 🍎

---

3 **struck the prey with his talons.** Yammer thinks the picture on TV is something (prey) he should hunt. He hits the screen with his claws (talons).

4 **otherworldly creature.** A being that is not from the human world

5 **Roger Tory Peterson field guides.** Books with pictures and descriptions of different kinds of wildlife

6 **preening his feathers.** Cleaning and trimming his feathers with his beak

1 What is this story mostly about?

Ⓐ the appearance and behavior of owls

Ⓑ a girl's collection of pets

Ⓒ a pet owl who likes TV

Ⓓ the bad effects of watching too much TV

2 What is a lesson you can learn from this story?

Ⓐ When you live with animals, they often act a lot like people.

Ⓑ Keeping wild animals as pets is very dangerous.

Ⓒ Watching TV improves your schoolwork.

Ⓓ All birds like to watch TV.

3 What items for Yammer are included on the family's shopping list?

Ⓐ ants and beetles

Ⓑ mice and crickets

Ⓒ bread and butter

Ⓓ seeds and nuts

The Screech Owl Who Liked Television 3

4 Where is Yammer's own little bedroom?

(A) in Twig's closet

(B) between some books in the living-room bookcase

(C) in a box under Twig's bed

(D) in a drawer lined with a blanket in Twig's room

5 Which event happens LAST?

(A) Yammer preens his feathers on top of Twig's open door.

(B) Yammer falls out of his nest.

(C) Yammer tries to hunt a horse on TV.

(D) The mother puts the TV up in her bedroom.

6 Why does Yammer crash into the TV screen?

(A) because he is trying to turn off the TV

(B) because he is angry and wants to break the TV

(C) because he can't fly very well

(D) because the horse looks like a mouse to him

7 When her mother tells Twig to stop watching TV, Twig gets to her feet reluctantly. What does *reluctantly* mean?

(A) unwillingly

(B) cheerfully

(C) painfully

(D) fearfully

8 Yammer strikes the TV screen and drops to the floor, bewildered. What does *bewildered* mean?

(A) thrilled

(B) confused

(C) convinced

(D) laughing

9 From what you know about Twig, how does she feel about wild animals?

(A) She is afraid of them.

(B) She thinks that they should be left alone.

(C) She believes that they have feelings.

(D) She thinks that they can learn to read.

10 What would Twig's mother be most likely to do if Twig brought home another hurt or hungry animal?

(A) She would tell Twig to let the animal go back to the wild.

(B) She would help Twig take care of the animal.

(C) She would make Twig take the animal to a neighbor's house.

(D) She would let the animal sleep in her own bed.

The Screech Owl Who Liked Television   5

LESSON 1

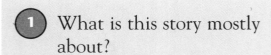

How to Answer Questions About Main Ideas

1 What is this story mostly about?

(A) the appearance and behavior of owls

(B) a girl's collection of pets

(C) a pet owl who likes TV

(D) the bad effects of watching too much TV

Step by Step

Question 1 asks about the main idea of the story. The **main idea** is what the whole story is mostly about. To find the main idea, you can skim the story. When you **skim,** you look over the whole story quickly. You should read the title and any special notes, like the editor's note on page 1. You should also read the first sentences of paragraphs and any words in special type. Once you get an idea of what the story is mainly about, try to sum up this idea in one sentence. Then read the whole story carefully.

The title of this story and the first line tell you that the story is about a special owl who likes TV. As you read, you will see that the story ends with the girl asking for permission to watch TV with the owl. You might decide that answer C, "a pet owl who likes TV," is the right answer.

To make sure that your answer is the *best* one, always check the other answers. For a main idea question, you should be sure that your answer talks about the *whole* story, not just part of it. For this question, answer A says, "the appearance and behavior of owls." You do learn something about how this owl looks and acts, but the story is not about all owls. You know from the first line that the girl does have several pets, but the story doesn't tell about her other pets. Therefore, you know that answer B is not the best one. The mother does not want Twig to watch too much TV, but nothing is said about the bad effects of it (answer D). By ruling out answers A, B, and D, you can see that C is, in fact, the right answer.

2 What is a lesson you can learn from this story?

(A) When you live with animals, they often act a lot like people.

(B) Keeping wild animals as pets is very dangerous.

(C) Watching TV improves your schoolwork.

(D) All birds like to watch TV.

Step by Step

Another kind of main idea question asks about a lesson in a story. A lesson taught by a story is called a **theme.**

The girl in this story likes to make friends with wild animals. It might be dangerous to keep *some* wild animals, but this story does not teach that it is dangerous to keep wild animals as pets (B). The story does not show that TV improves your schoolwork, so C is not a good answer. Yammer does like to watch TV, but the story doesn't teach that *all* birds like to watch TV (D).

What about answer A? The story says, "Yammer had become a person to Twig, who felt all wild friends were humans and should be treated as such." The story says that Yammer likes activities that people like, such as watching TV. The story shows that "this otherworldly creature was a person" by telling that his dinner is included on the shopping list and that he has his own bedroom. Finally, the story makes a statement much like answer A: "When you live with animals, they often seem quite humanlike."

Tips

📖 Look for key words in the question that tell you it is asking about the main idea. This kind of question may use such key words as *main idea, theme, lesson, as a whole, mostly,* or *for the most part.*

📖 Begin by reading *all* the answers. Rule out any that are obviously wrong. Then concentrate on the answers that are left.

📖 Remember that a statement can be true but still not tell the main idea. Make sure that the answer you choose is true *and* that it tells the most important idea of the whole story.

📖 A question about the main idea can be asked in many ways. It might ask for the main idea, for the theme, or for another title for the selection. It might ask what lesson is being taught or what the selection is mostly about.

LESSON 2

How to Answer Questions About Details

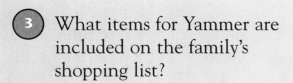

3 What items for Yammer are included on the family's shopping list?

A ants and beetles

B mice and crickets

C bread and butter

D seeds and nuts

Step by Step

Question 3 does not ask about a big idea in the story. Instead, it asks about a small point, or **detail.** Sometimes details help to support the main idea.

To find answers to questions about details, you can scan. When you **scan,** you move your eyes quickly down the page to find the information that you need. It might help to run your finger or a ruler down the page and follow it with your eyes.

To scan for an answer about a detail, pick a key word or key phrase from the question. Find one or more words that you think will lead you to the answer. That is your **key word** or **key phrase.** Try to pick a word that does not appear too often. *Yammer*

would not be a good key word. It appears all through the story and not just near the information that you need to answer the question.

For this question, you could look for the key phrase *shopping list.* Now scan the selection, looking for the key phrase. When you find the key phrase, read the sentences around it. The sentence with this phrase in it says, "Wasn't his menu of mice and crickets included on the shopping list?" Now you know that B, "mice and crickets," is the correct answer.

4 Where is Yammer's own little bedroom?

   Ⓐ in Twig's closet

   Ⓑ between some books in the living-room bookcase

   Ⓒ in a box under Twig's bed

   Ⓓ in a drawer lined with a blanket in Twig's room

Step by Step

To find the answer for question 4, you might choose the key word *bedroom* from the question. If you scan the selection for the word *bedroom*, you find it first in the paragraph at the top of page 2. The paragraph is about the mother's bedroom, so you need to keep looking.

About halfway down the page, you find the word again. This sentence reads, "Didn't he have his own bedroom in the gap between the Roger Tory Peterson field guides in the living room bookcase?" If you don't know what the "Roger Tory Peterson field guides" are, you can check the footnote. A small number following a word tells you that the word is explained at the bottom of the page in a **footnote.** This footnote tells you that the field guides are books. Yammer's "bedroom" is in the gap, or space, between some books in the living-room bookcase, answer B.

Tips

📖 To find a particular detail, scan the passage for a key word or phrase. Then read closely to find the answer you need.

📖 Use your finger, an index card, or a ruler to keep your place as you scan down a page.

📖 Sometimes you will need to keep scanning to find the key word for the information you need.

LESSON 3

How to Answer Questions About Sequence

5 Which event happens LAST?

A Yammer preens his feathers on top of Twig's open door.

B Yammer falls out of his nest.

C Yammer tries to hunt a horse on TV.

D The mother puts the TV up in her bedroom.

Step by Step

As you read, notice when the events take place. The order in which events happen is called **sequence.** A sequence question might ask which event occurs *first* or *last.* It might ask which event happens *before* or *after* other events.

Question 5 asks which event happens last. To answer the question, go over the order of events. First, Yammer falls out of his nest, so he comes to live with Twig's family. After he has been part of the family for a while, he and Twig watch a cowboy show on television. They watch in Twig's mother's bedroom. Twig's mother had put a TV in there earlier.

"Later that morning," the owl perches on top of Twig's door, preening his feathers. Now you know that the last of these events is answer A, "Yammer preens his feathers on top of Twig's open door."

Notice the word *later.* This word is a clue that tells you when something happens. Other words that give you clues about sequence are *first, next, then, before, after,* and *finally.*

Stories often tell events in the order that they happen. Be careful, because writers sometimes tell events out of order. They might tell you something that happened earlier or mention something that will happen later.

Tips

📖 Remember that events are often, *but not always,* told in order in a story.

📖 Look for key words like *first, next, later, before, after,* and *last,* both in the story and in the questions.

📖 Notice dates and times.

📖 Words that tell about times or seasons are also clues. Examples: "One Saturday morning"; "Before the green of June"

How to Answer Questions About Cause and Effect

6 Why does Yammer crash into the TV screen?

Ⓐ because he is trying to turn off the TV

Ⓑ because he is angry and wants to break the TV

Ⓒ because he can't fly very well

Ⓓ because the horse looks like a mouse to him

Step by Step

Questions with the word *why* are usually asking you to tell the cause of something. A **cause** is a reason or thing that makes something happen. An **effect** is the result that happens. For example, a dropped match might *cause* a forest fire. The fire is the *effect* of the dropped match.

This question asks you what causes Yammer to crash into the TV screen. To find the answer, read the passage carefully. The story does not say that Yammer is angry or that he wants to turn off the TV. We don't know how well he can fly. The story does say that Yammer is watching a cowboy show on TV. He is staring at the screen, where he sees a horse and rider "streaking across the desert." The next sentence gives you a clue to what Yammer is thinking: "From an owl's point of view the pair were mouse-sized." Then Yammer pushes off from the headboard, strikes what he thinks is the "prey," and drops to the floor. Now you know that Yammer flies at the screen because he wants to hunt something that he thinks is a mouse.

Tips

📖 Look for key words, such as *cause, because, effect, why, reason, therefore, as a result,* and *so.*

📖 Remember that one event can *follow* another without being caused by it. Something is a cause only if it makes something else happen. Example: Joe finished his homework. Then dinner was ready. This does not show cause and effect.

LESSON 5

How to Answer Questions About Vocabulary

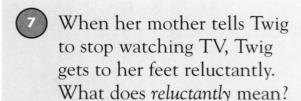

7 When her mother tells Twig to stop watching TV, Twig gets to her feet reluctantly. What does *reluctantly* mean?

Ⓐ unwillingly

Ⓑ cheerfully

Ⓒ painfully

Ⓓ fearfully

Step by Step

A common kind of multiple-choice question asks about the meaning of a word. If you see an unfamiliar word standing by itself, you have no way of knowing what the word means. If you see this word in a story, however, you may be able to figure out its meaning from the context. The **context** of a word is the words that come before and after it. The context can give you hints that help you to figure out the word's meaning. These hints are called **context clues.**

To figure out what *reluctantly* means, you can look at clues in the story that show Twig's attitude. The story says that Twig and Yammer have been watching TV for hours. Twig's mother comes to tell Twig that she has watched TV long enough. She tells her to go and do something else. Twig reluctantly gets up to leave, but she turns back and looks at her little owl. She pouts and complains, "How come Yammer can watch TV and I can't?" These words and actions let us know that Twig is not pleased. She is not happy about going to do something else, so answer B is wrong. She is not hurt, so answer C is incorrect, too. She is not afraid, so we can rule out answer D. Only answer A, "unwillingly," makes sense in the context of this story.

8 Yammer strikes the TV screen and drops to the floor, bewildered. What does *bewildered* mean?

- (A) thrilled
- (B) confused
- (C) convinced
- (D) laughing

Step by Step

Bewildered is another word that might not be familiar to you. You can figure out its meaning by noticing how it is used in the story. In this case, the word is used to describe the little owl after he crashes into the TV set. First of all, you can rule out answers A and D. You know that Yammer is not laughing or thrilled because he would not be happy about flying into a TV screen. Which one of the other answers is the best? The narrator tells you that Yammer thinks the horse with its rider is a mouse. Yammer flies at the TV, expecting to catch the "mouse," but, instead, he runs into the hard screen and drops onto the floor. The owl is not convinced about anything. In fact, he has found out that he was wrong. You can imagine that he is feeling shocked and mixed-up because something very unexpected has happened. The context tells us that the best answer is B, "confused."

Tips

Keep a vocabulary journal. Write down new words that you learn, along with their definitions. Study your list to build your vocabulary.

When you see an unfamiliar word, read the context for clues to its meaning.

Key words such as *also* and *as* may show how words are alike: "Tyrone was infuriated, and Jesse was also angry."

Key words such as *but, rather,* and *on the other hand* may point out words with opposite meanings: "Leandro is elated, but Dahlia is sad."

Watch for restatements that define a word by repeating the idea again in different words: "Astronomy, or the study of stars, is interesting."

LESSON 6

How to Answer Questions That Ask You to Make a Guess

9 From what you know about Twig, how does she feel about wild animals?

- Ⓐ She is afraid of them.

- Ⓑ She thinks that they should be left alone.

- Ⓒ She believes that they have feelings.

- Ⓓ She thinks that they can learn to read.

Step by Step

If you read through the possible answers for question 9, you will see that not one of these statements is made in the story. To answer this question, you have to figure out something about Twig by noticing what she says and does. When you guess about something that is not clearly stated, you are making an **inference.**

The story says that Twig believes "all wild friends [are] humans." She lets her owl watch TV. She cuddles him when he crashes into the TV set. She makes "cozy blanket-tunnels" for him, which causes him to "utter his note of contentment." Finally, she says, "I feel sorry for Yammer." She thinks that he needs to see things move the way they do in the woods.

As you think about these facts, you can safely guess that Twig is not afraid of wild animals (A). She certainly does not think they should be left alone (B). She brings them home, plays with them, and makes them her friends. Answer D is not a sensible answer; even if Twig believes animals are like people in some ways, she doesn't try to teach them to read. The best answer is C, "She believes that they have feelings." Twig shows that she thinks that wild animals like Yammer are happy when their needs are met and sad when they can't have what they want.

10 What would Twig's mother be most likely to do if Twig brought home another hurt or hungry animal?

Ⓐ She would tell Twig to let the animal go back to the wild.

Ⓑ She would help Twig take care of the animal.

Ⓒ She would make Twig take the animal to a neighbor's house.

Ⓓ She would let the animal sleep in her own bed.

Step by Step

Question 10 asks you to make a guess about what might happen if Twig brought home another animal. When you guess what might happen, you are making a **prediction.**

To answer this question, you need to know something about Twig's mother. It seems that Twig's mother lets her keep the animals that she finds; Yammer is an example of how their wild pets become part of the family. Like Twig, her mother has a soft spot for these animals. She says that Yammer has made himself dear to the family. His foods are on the family's shopping list. She even lets him sit at the dining table. At the end of the story, she gives in and lets Twig and Yammer watch TV together. There is no hint that the mother would make Twig take the animal to a neighbor's home (C) or back to the wild (A). We don't see the mother letting animals sleep in her bed (D); Yammer has his own little bedroom in the bookcase. From these facts, you can figure out that the best answer is B, "She would help Twig take care of the animal."

Tips

📖 Base your inferences and predictions on facts that you do know.

📖 Try to rule out as many wrong answers as possible. Then use reasoning to pick the best answer from those that remain.

📖 Sometimes, you can reason from a general statement to make a specific guess. If the story says that Twig loves animals, you can guess that she loves Yammer.

📖 Sometimes you can reason from specific facts to a general rule. If the story says Twig feeds Yammer, cuddles Yammer, and plays with Yammer, you can guess that Twig cares about Yammer's needs.

DIRECTIONS

Read this story about some unusual animals. Then answer questions 1 through 10.

An okapi

Unusual Creatures
by Malik Hanson

When you go to a zoo, you expect to see giraffes, elephants, and monkeys. There are lots of other animals in the zoo (and in the world, too). Have you ever heard of the okapi or the coatimundi? These are just two of the world's less famous creatures.

The okapi looks like a cross between a zebra and a donkey. Its closest relative, however, is the giraffe. The okapi is black, with black-and-white stripes on its legs and backside. Its color and stripes help it to hide in bushes. Because the okapi can hide well and run quickly, scientists don't know much about it. They do know that okapis have very long tongues so that they can pull down leaves from trees to eat. They also use their tongues, which are blue and black, to clean their eyes and ears!

Suppose someone asked you to draw a picture of a coatimundi. What would you draw? This interesting animal, also known as the white-nosed coati, is a member of the raccoon family. Coatis are about the same size as raccoons, but they have long snouts, or noses. Coatis are brownish red with white noses and white streaks that go across their nose and eyes. The coati also has stripes on its tail. Coatis like to swim. They live in the trees at night and on the ground during the day. Female coatis often travel in groups, while male coatis like to be alone. When a coati is surprised, it may jump into the trees while making clicking and woofing noises. Coatimundis live in Central America, and they are especially common in Belize.

You may have heard of the Tasmanian devil. It lives on the island of Tasmania in Australia. This animal is about the size of a small dog. The second part of its name comes from the scary sound that it makes at night, especially if it is feeding or fighting with another animal. You may see a picture of a Tasmanian devil with its mouth open, looking as if it is mad. This animal is actually fairly shy. It bares its teeth in fear. Tasmanian devils sleep in logs or caves during the day and wake up at night.

These animals have very strong teeth. They can chomp through animal bones easily. A Tasmanian devil can eat about half of what it weighs in half an hour! Tasmanian devils almost became extinct. Now they are protected by law.

Another unusual animal is the nine-banded armadillo. This armadillo is about the size of a cat. It has a hard shell that helps to protect it from other animals. There are several species of armadillo, all of which live in South America. The nine-banded armadillo migrated, or moved, to America. It is most common in Texas, where it is the official state mammal. This animal needs to live in warm areas where it can dig in the soil. It likes to dig for grubs and bugs to eat. The armadillo can smell bugs that are as deep as six inches underground. They can also swim by blowing themselves up with air. They inhale so much air that they double in size. This allows them to float in the water! The funniest thing about armadillos is that when they are surprised by something, they jump three feet into the air!

It is fun to learn about unusual animals. Who knows? Someday you might be driving along when you see a creature jump high off the ground. When everyone else shouts, "What *was* that?" you will be able to say, "Oh, that? That was just a startled armadillo, of course!" 🍎

A coatimundi

1 What happens FIRST?

    Ⓐ The armadillo wants to cross a river.

    Ⓑ The armadillo breathes in a large amount of air.

    Ⓒ The armadillo begins to float.

    Ⓓ The armadillo doubles in size.

This is a sequence question.

2 What is another good title for this selection?

    Ⓐ "Science in the Desert"

    Ⓑ "Cruel Animals"

    Ⓒ "Interesting Animals of the Wild"

    Ⓓ "How Armadillos Swim"

This question asks about the main idea.

3 Where do coatis live?

    Ⓐ Australia

    Ⓑ Texas

    Ⓒ Belize

    Ⓓ Africa

This is a question about a detail.

4 The nine-banded armadillo migrated to Texas. What does *migrated* mean?

    Ⓐ flew

    Ⓑ moved

    Ⓒ drove

    Ⓓ swam

This is a vocabulary question.

5 Which of the following words best describes the okapi?

    (A) quick

    (B) slow

    (C) green

    (D) dirty

6 If you saw a coati traveling by itself in the wild, what might you guess about it?

    (A) It is probably sleepy.

    (B) It is probably male.

    (C) It is probably female.

    (D) It is probably hungry.

7 What is one effect of the okapi having a long tongue?

    (A) It often bites its tongue by mistake.

    (B) It can use it to clean its ears.

    (C) The tongue falls out of its mouth most of the time.

    (D) It scares other creatures away.

8 What causes armadillos to jump high into the air?

   Ⓐ They get very happy.

   Ⓑ They get very angry.

   Ⓒ They get itchy.

   Ⓓ They get surprised.

This question asks about cause and effect.

9 How did the Tasmanian devil get its name?

   Ⓐ because of its size

   Ⓑ because it makes scary sounds when it eats

   Ⓒ because it has strong teeth

   Ⓓ because of its nose

This question asks about cause and effect.

10 Before they swim, armadillos inhale air. What does *inhale* mean?

   Ⓐ blow out

   Ⓑ breathe in

   Ⓒ stir up

   Ⓓ give up

This is a vocabulary question.

A Tasmanian devil

DIRECTIONS

Read this story about a human-built wonder.
Then answer questions 1 through 10.

The Great Wall of China
by Morgan Williamson

The Great Wall of China is a long, high wall that stretches along the northern part of the country. Over two thousand years ago, the first emperor of China, Shihuangdi, designed the wall. He wanted to keep out enemies and to protect the country from attacks. Many emperors after that added to the wall over the years, making it longer and higher. For hundreds of years, the wall was renovated, rebuilt, and fixed. Now the Great Wall of China stands as one of the most wonderful constructions ever built by human beings.

The first part of the Great Wall was constructed during the rule of the first emperor. Under this emperor's leadership, workers built the wall 1,200 miles long. The work took about 17 years. This first section of the wall was made mostly of stone.

Later, Emperor Wu-Di repaired the first emperor's crumbling wall. Then he added another 300 miles of wall, crossing the harsh Gobi Desert. In order to build a wall that could withstand the hot, dry desert, his workers made wooden frames and added a layer of strong willow branches at the bottom. Then they poured in a mixture of water and gravel. After the mixture dried, workers took off the frames, leaving solid slabs.

When Yuanzhang became emperor, his workers developed a special type of brick to use for the wall. They heated the bricks in a kiln, or oven. The heat made the bricks stronger. These bricks also lasted longer than the blocks used before. What is more, these special bricks were easy to make, and the wall could be built more quickly.

The emperors who ruled during the next 275 years expanded the wall. They connected the larger walls with smaller ones miles away. They also constructed towers and forts where guards could watch for approaching enemies. Sometimes guards made tall columns of smoke on the wall to warn of an attack. The number of smoke signals told people how many soldiers were coming. At night, the guards made signals with fire.

It was during these 275 years, from 1368–1644, that most of the Great Wall was constructed. If you took all the stones that were added to the wall in this one period, you could build a wall that would reach all the way around the globe! At that time, close to one million soldiers guarded the wall, and it was successful in keeping out enemies.

The Great Wall of China is now about 4,500 miles long. That is about the distance from Miami, Florida, to the North Pole. Some parts of the wall are old and falling apart, while other areas have remained strong. The main part of the wall is about twenty-five feet high. It is about twenty feet wide at the base, or bottom. The Great Wall of China is so large that it can be seen from the moon! It is the only object made by human beings that can be seen from space. Today the wall attracts visitors from all around the world who want to walk along the wall and explore the history of China. 🍎

1 What is this article mostly about?

   (A) how the Great Wall of China was built

   (B) hiking on the Great Wall of China

   (C) how China was divided into parts

   (D) the distance from Miami to the North Pole

2 Whose workers used ovens to bake strong bricks?

   (A) the last emperor

   (B) the first emperor

   (C) Emperor Yuanzhang

   (D) Emperor Wu-Di

3 The Great Wall of China was built

   (A) to protect China from enemies.

   (B) because there was nothing else to do.

   (C) so people could see it from space.

   (D) to help travelers cross the desert.

4 Which event happened FIRST?

   (A) The Great Wall of China was seen from the moon.

   (B) Dirt and stone were used to build the wall.

   (C) Brick was used to build the wall.

   (D) A million soldiers guarded the wall.

5 A smoke signal from the wall meant

(A) it was time to change guards.

(B) enemies were attacking.

(C) the wall was broken.

(D) it was about to rain.

6 When there was an attack at night,

(A) guards made signals with fire.

(B) soldiers used smoke signals as warnings.

(C) soldiers turned on the lights.

(D) the dirt wall fell down.

7 Emperor Wu-Di wanted to build a wall that could withstand the hot, dry desert. What does *withstand* mean?

(A) encourage

(B) heat up

(C) build with

(D) stay strong in

8 If you went to visit the Great Wall of China, you

   Ⓐ might help to build the wall, assisted by other tourists from around the world.

   Ⓑ might learn about Chinese history.

   Ⓒ might see fires burning to warn of an attack.

   Ⓓ could walk along the wall from end to end in one day.

9 For hundreds of years, the wall was renovated, rebuilt, and fixed. What does *renovate* mean?

   Ⓐ make like new

   Ⓑ break in half

   Ⓒ ignore

   Ⓓ write stories about

10 The Great Wall of China is so big, it can be seen from

   Ⓐ all around the world.

   Ⓑ the North Pole.

   Ⓒ Miami, Florida.

   Ⓓ the moon.

Archway in the Great Wall

DIRECTIONS

Read this story about a girl whose father runs a diner. Then answer questions 1 through 10.

June's Tuesday Special
by Alejandra Martínez

While most fourth-graders ran around the playground after school ended, June did not have time to play with her classmates. Today, like every other day after school, she ran down to the Franklin Street Diner.

"How was school, sweetie?" June's father asked. He had a pencil stuck behind his ear, and he was wearing a big apron with orange stains on it. He had four steaming plates balanced on his forearms.

Today was June's favorite day of the week—Tuesday. Almost everyone liked Fridays, but June always loved Tuesday because it was Delivery Day.

"Delivery Day, Dad!" June smiled brightly. "Can I sign for it? Please?"

June's father grinned back. "Of course you can sign. Go help Sal and Christina in the back."

"Hello there, Joo-Joo," Christina said, "do you want to sign for the deliveries?" Christina and Sal were carrying big boxes of vegetables into the kitchen. Someone had to sign a paper to say the diner had received its whole order of food. The delivery person handed June a clipboard with an important-looking piece of paper on it. June carefully signed her name at the bottom.

June was busy the rest of the day. She set tables, wiped off the counters, and even made sure the jukebox was always playing. When things quieted down,

June sat down at the biggest table in the diner and started her homework.

The next day June was in class when she had a sudden thought. She realized that she had left her homework at the diner. June went to the office and called her dad. He told her not to worry. He would drive by and drop off her homework.

When her class was out on the playground, June's father pulled up to the school. June's classmates saw a big man with a thick moustache and a big apron with gravy splotches and soup stains splattered all over it. The man handed June her homework and gave her a quick hug.

As her father drove away with a wave and a smile, June heard giggles.

"Did you see that guy? Can you believe he's June's *dad?*" Matthew cried.

"What about his apron?" Joanna asked.

"It was so dirty! Gross!" Joanna pinched her nose and cringed.

June turned purple with anger. "Don't make fun of my dad!" June cried. "He's more important than all of you put together. He runs a very special diner, and I help him." June glared at Matthew and Joanna. "Obviously," June added proudly, "you haven't been to the Franklin Street Diner." She held her head high and walked away.

"Who cares about a stupid diner anyway?" Matthew scoffed. Joanna rolled her eyes.

After school, June and her friend Miranda went to the diner. June's father greeted the girls with a grin. He had a new menu in his hand. "This is to thank you for all your work," he said to June. He opened the menu and pointed.

June read aloud, "June's Tuesday Special: Turkey breast sandwich with lettuce, tomatoes, pickles, and onions; small salad; and juice." June's grin stretched from ear to ear.

"Wow, your own special!" Miranda said.

"I can't believe it," exclaimed June. "Everyone who comes here will order it!"

Smiles and laughter filled the diner. Sal and Christina congratulated June. It didn't matter if some kids at school thought the diner was stupid. June was famous! 🍎

1 Why doesn't June have time to play with her classmates after school?

(A) She works at her father's diner.

(B) She goes to cooking lessons.

(C) She delivers food.

(D) She has to fix the jukebox.

2 June's father is wearing an apron with gravy splotches splattered all over it. What is a *splotch*?

(A) a hole

(B) a stain

(C) a pocket

(D) a picture

3 What is this story mostly about?

(A) a girl who enjoys working at a diner

(B) classmates who might become friends

(C) a special apron

(D) children who help their parents

4 Which do you think would be the best word to describe June?

- (A) tearful
- (B) lazy
- (C) proud
- (D) bored

5 What causes Joanna to pinch her nose and cringe?

- (A) She smells onions in her lunch.
- (B) She thinks about the dirty apron.
- (C) She learns that June has a special named after her.
- (D) She sees the Franklin Street Diner.

6 What happens AFTER June walks away from Matthew and Joanna?

- (A) June's father drops off her homework.
- (B) June's father drives away.
- (C) June signs for the delivery.
- (D) June and Miranda go to the diner.

7 Why does June sign for the delivery?

(A) because someone needs to say that the diner has received its whole order

(B) because her name is on the "special"

(C) because she is the only one who can write

(D) because she has done all her homework

8 What is one task June does at the diner?

(A) She cooks food.

(B) She serves customers.

(C) She sets tables.

(D) She fills the ketchup bottles.

9 What is the theme of this story?

(A) It doesn't matter what other people think, as long as you like what you do.

(B) People should not get messy while they are working.

(C) Your name might appear in a menu.

(D) Friday is the best day of the week.

10 From what we can see in the story, it seems that June's father is

(A) very loving.

(B) too busy to help her.

(C) a terrible cook.

(D) an English teacher.

DIRECTIONS

Read this story about what happens when a person breaks a bone. Then answer questions 1 through 10.

Down to the Bone

by Melinda Hsieh

Randall was happily riding down his street on his new bike. Suddenly, he lost control and crashed into a fence. He scraped his hands and knees badly and bruised his legs. When he sat up, Randall realized he couldn't move his right wrist or hand. He felt a lot of pain, and his arm was swollen and red. Randall's parents took him to the emergency room. After looking at the X-rays, the doctor told Randall that he had **fractured,** or broken, his arm.

About six million fractures happen in the United States every year. On average, each of us can expect to fracture about two bones in a lifetime. Accidents can happen anywhere, from the ski slopes to the bathtub. Luckily, most people's bodies can successfully repair fractures.

When you break a bone, blood begins to thicken, or **clot,** around the area to stop the bleeding. Then, a material called **collagen** begins to form between the pieces of broken bone. The collagen grows to join the separated pieces of bone together. As time passes, **osteoblasts,** or cells that make bone, form a layer, like a sponge over the collagen. Finally, harder bone replaces the spongy layer, and the fracture is healed. Depending on how badly the bone is broken, it takes from one to three months for it to heal. Older people take longer to heal. Adult bones take about twice as long as children's bones to heal. If a fracture is severe—that is, if the bone is very badly broken—it can take over six months to heal!

Randall's doctor made sure that his arm would heal properly. First, she **set** his fracture by carefully straightening his arm. Then the doctor wrapped his arm snugly in a cast. A **cast** is made with strips of plastic, fiberglass, or plaster that are wrapped around the broken body part. Casts keep the bone straight and immobilized, or unable to move. If the arm was not set straight and kept straight, the broken ends of the bone might join in a crooked way, which could lead to future problems. The doctor told Randall to get a lot of rest and not to get the cast wet. By following his doctor's orders, Randall recovered completely and started riding his bike again.

Sometimes, people with severely fractured bones need more than a cast to help them heal. Doctors may have to put in screws, rods, and pins to hold the broken bone in place.

Today, scientists are working on another way to treat broken bones. Doctors are creating a new substance called bone paste, which is like glue. Bone paste can be put into a needle and shot into the broken bone. The paste turns into a material like bone and heals the fracture. People who developed this paste say it takes about ten minutes for the paste to harden and about twelve hours for the paste to become as good as bone. Scientists are still testing bone paste to make sure that it is successful and safe for people.

One way to prevent broken bones is to keep them healthy and strong. By eating foods that are high in calcium, like milk and yogurt, you can build stronger bones. In fact, 99 percent of the calcium in your body goes to making bones stronger and healthier. If your bones don't get enough calcium, you can develop **osteoporosis,** a condition that makes bones weak and brittle, or easy to break. Exercise also helps to strengthen your bones. By making your bones healthy now, you can save yourself a lot of pain later! 🍎

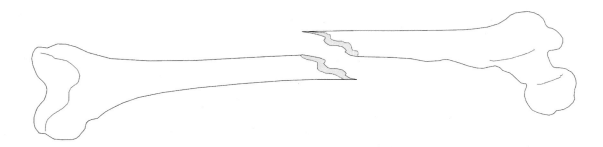

1 What are osteoblasts?

   (A) paste to replace broken bones

   (B) cells that make bone

   (C) a condition that makes bones weak

   (D) a doctor who fixes broken bones

2 What happens FIRST?

   (A) The broken bone is wrapped in a cast.

   (B) Collagen forms in the fracture.

   (C) Blood clots around the broken bone.

   (D) The broken bone heals.

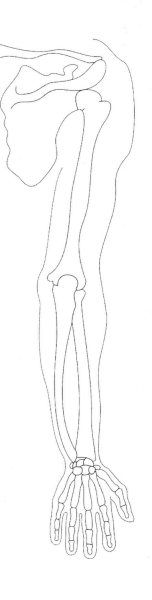

3 What might happen if you got osteoporosis?

   (A) You might need to stop drinking milk.

   (B) You might need to go on vacation.

   (C) You might cough and sneeze easily.

   (D) You might break bones easily.

4 What is the main idea of the selection?

   (A) With proper care, broken bones can be healed and prevented.

   (B) Casts cannot get wet.

   (C) Milk can help your bones grow big and strong.

   (D) Bone paste might be a new way to treat fractures.

5 What is one effect caused by a broken bone?

(A) brittle bones

(B) thinner blood

(C) swelling

(D) spongy bones

6 The article says that doctors put casts around broken bones to keep them immobilized. What does *immobilized* mean?

(A) brittle

(B) in pain

(C) unable to move

(D) unable to be healed

7 What happened BEFORE the doctor put Randall's broken arm in a cast?

(A) The doctor straightened his arm.

(B) The doctor told Randall to rest.

(C) Randall's arm was healed.

(D) Randall got his cast wet.

8 According to the article, how many fractures happen in the United States every year?

- Ⓐ about six thousand
- Ⓑ about six trillion
- Ⓒ about six million
- Ⓓ about nine million

9 Broken bones are

- Ⓐ a sign that you need more sleep.
- Ⓑ painful, but they can be healed.
- Ⓒ always caused by skiing accidents.
- Ⓓ not fixable.

10 The article says that a severe fracture can take over six months to heal. What does *severe* mean in this article?

- Ⓐ very bad
- Ⓑ very weak
- Ⓒ very spongy
- Ⓓ very red

Down to the Bone 35

DIRECTIONS

Read this story about an American hero.
Then answer questions 1 through 10.

Sacagawea and baby, as
pictured on a gold coin issued
by the U.S. government

Sacagawea's Journey
by Barnes P. Wentworth

In 1803, the United States bought a large piece of land from France for fifteen million dollars. Called the Louisiana Purchase, this deal made the United States twice as big as it had been before. President Thomas Jefferson sent a group of people to explore this new land. The explorers planned to travel on the Missouri and Columbia Rivers. They would study the climate, geography, plants and animals, and the language and customs of the Native Americans who lived in this land.

In 1804, Meriwether Lewis and William Clark set out to see the new land. They hired Toussaint Charbonneau as a translator. He was a fur trader who spoke French and Hidatsa, a Native-American language. The explorers also wanted the fur trader's wife, Sacagawea, to travel with their group. Sacagawea spoke Hidatsa and Shoshone, another Native-American language. Lewis and Clark needed Sacagawea to help them make friends with Native Americans they met on their journey.

Sacagawea was a member of the Shoshone nation. She had been kidnapped by the Hidatsa, who were enemies of the Shoshone. Her captors took her from her home when she was a young girl and sold her as a slave. When she met the explorers, she was married to Charbonneau. Two months before beginning her journey, Sacagawea gave birth to a son, Jean-Baptiste Charbonneau.

Sacagawea, her baby, and her husband set off with Lewis and Clark on the Missouri River. In addition to Sacagawea's other duties, she dug for roots and found berries and plants that the explorers could eat. Sacagawea carried Jean-Baptiste on a cradleboard. A **cradleboard** is a flat piece of wood that a mother straps to her back. The baby is wrapped snugly against the board and can look around as its mother travels. She played with her son on the boat. He danced and bounced. Clark nicknamed the baby "Pomp" or "Pompy."

In May of 1805, the boat that carried Sacagawea was turned over by a strong wind. Sacagawea helped to save many important papers and supplies that would have been lost if she hadn't acted quickly. Lewis and Clark were very grateful for her help.

In August of 1805, the explorers arrived at the Shoshone lands. When Sacagawea met with the chief to buy horses, she discovered that the chief was her brother! Though she could have stayed behind with her people, she helped to buy the horses and continued the exploration.

Along the journey, Sacagawea was also helpful. Sometimes the explorers met Native Americans who had never seen white settlers before. Sacagawea helped to explain to these people that Lewis and Clark were friendly explorers.

On the journey home, Sacagawea led the group along many trails that she had known as a young girl. Clark praised her, calling her their "pilot." She led the expedition safely back to their camp. In 1806, Sacagawea's journey ended. She received nothing for her efforts, but her husband received $500.33 and 320 acres of land.

Sacagawea died in 1812, at the age of 25, from a fever. Before she died, she had another baby, a daughter she named Lisette. William Clark, who had grown quite fond of Jean-Baptiste, adopted both Lisette and Jean-Baptiste.

Sacagawea helped Lewis and Clark to explore the new territory peacefully. She guided them along trails and helped to preserve important papers. She communicated with the Native Americans. Sacagawea earned a place in history as a famous explorer of the North American continent. 🍎

Map of North America

1 Which of the following events happened FIRST?

(A) The United States made the Louisiana Purchase.

(B) Sacagawea's son rode in a cradleboard.

(C) Sacagawea translated for Lewis and Clark.

(D) Sacagawea's daughter was born.

2 What was a result of Sacagawea's travels with Lewis and Clark?

(A) Many Native-American nations became angry.

(B) The explorers were able to buy horses.

(C) Sacagawea and her husband were separated.

(D) They were able to sail on the Pacific Ocean.

3 What might be another good title for this article?

(A) "Sacagawea's Children"

(B) "Sacagawea the Explorer"

(C) "Lewis and Clark Explore the West"

(D) "Sacagawea and the Shoshone"

4 What is one language the story says Toussaint Charbonneau could speak?

(A) English

(B) French

(C) Shoshone

(D) Iroquois

Meriwether Lewis

5 Sacagawea's captors kidnapped her when she was a young girl. What are *captors*?

    Ⓐ people who give tours

    Ⓑ people who take someone prisoner

    Ⓒ people who lived long ago

    Ⓓ people who explore new territory

6 What was one of Sacagawea's duties?

    Ⓐ digging for treasure

    Ⓑ making maps

    Ⓒ finding roots and berries

    Ⓓ cooking for everyone

7 What might have happened if Sacagawea hadn't acted quickly when the boat turned over?

    Ⓐ Important papers would have been lost.

    Ⓑ Lewis and Clark would have left her behind.

    Ⓒ The Shoshone nation would have been disappointed.

    Ⓓ Jean-Baptiste wouldn't have traveled with her anymore.

William Clark

8 What is the main idea of this article?

(A) Sacagawea was a member of the Shoshone nation.

(B) Toussaint Charbonneau was a fur trader.

(C) Thomas Jefferson was the third president of the United States.

(D) Sacagawea explored the Louisiana territory with Lewis and Clark.

9 What caused William Clark to call Sacagawea their "pilot?"

(A) She discovered new lands.

(B) She flew a plane over the Midwest.

(C) She guided the group.

(D) She steered the boat.

10 What happened AFTER Sacagawea led the group back to their camp?

(A) Sacagawea looked for berries.

(B) Toussaint was paid and given land.

(C) Jean-Baptiste was born.

(D) Members of the Hidatsa nation kidnapped Sacagawea.

The Mississippi

DIRECTIONS

Read this poem about an unusual vegetable.
Then answer questions 1 through 10.

The Farmer and the Beet
by Annie Sun Choi

There once was a farmer, a very poor man,
Who had a few seeds and a small plot of land.
"I'm hungry," he said with a terrible sigh,
"I think I'll give this small beet seed a try."

He hoed a small hole and dropped in the seed.
"Start growing," he said, "for I have a great need."
"I'm hungry, you see. My pantry is bare.
To a yummy beet sandwich naught else can compare!"

In time the small beet seed grew up toward the sun.
The beet kept growing till it weighed half a ton!
It was huge when it finally came to a stop,
And the farmer, poor fellow, looked up to the top.

He grabbed one big leaf. He pulled and he pried.
It wouldn't be plucked, however he tried!
"Oh, how can I harvest this humongous veggie?"
He called to his wife, a stout woman named Peggy.

The wife came on over to help out the man.
"Peggy," he said, "Pull as hard as you can!"
The Farmer and Peggy just couldn't win.
That's when the little dog Lucy stepped in.

The Farmer and Peggy and Lucy held tight.
Together they struggled with all of their might,
But the beet didn't budge, not even a tad,
So Bess the cow came and gave all she had.

But the beet didn't move. It just stood there still.
So Potter the Pony came over the hill.
"Oh, no!" Potter cried, "What a stubborn old beet!"
Then Sheep came to help, with a stomp and a bleat.

Still all of them failed; the beet didn't move,
It seemed that that beet had something to prove.
Did they pluck it? Dislodge it? Did it budge after that?
Of course it did not, so they called on the Cat.

And finally—POP! Out came the beet!
The delicious, nutritious, unbeatable treat!

"We did it! We picked it!" cried Peggy with cheer.
Lucy was beaming and shed happy tears,
Bess was ecstatic, and Potter was too,
The Sheep gave a leap, and the Cat almost flew.
A Rat who'd been watching this said with a squeal,
"We're all going to have such a wonderful meal!"
After chasing that lazy rat far, far away,
The Farmer got up and had something to say:
"Thank you, dear friends, for all your assistance.
Thank you again, for all your persistence.
You stayed and you pulled right down to the end.
Indeed, you are all my most generous friends!"
Joy filled the air. They awaited the day
When all would sit down to a big beet buffet. 🍎

1. What is the theme of the poem?

   Ⓐ Lucy is a good dog.

   Ⓑ A big job can be easier with help from friends.

   Ⓒ Beets are nutritious vegetables.

   Ⓓ Farming is hard work, but it is worth it.

2. Which of these events is most likely to happen after the events that occur in the poem?

   Ⓐ Bess and Potter the Pony will argue.

   Ⓑ Everyone will make fun of the Rat.

   Ⓒ The Farmer and Peggy will cook a beet feast.

   Ⓓ The friends will pick another beet.

3. Who came to help with "a stomp and a bleat?"

   Ⓐ Potter the Pony

   Ⓑ Cat

   Ⓒ Lucy

   Ⓓ Sheep

The Farmer and the Beet 43

4 The poem says that Bess and Potter are both ecstatic. What does *ecstatic* mean?

   Ⓐ very happy

   Ⓑ very angry

   Ⓒ very hungry

   Ⓓ very little

5 What causes the Farmer to plant his seed?

   Ⓐ He is bored.

   Ⓑ He is hungry.

   Ⓒ He is doing what his wife asked.

   Ⓓ He is doing what his friends do.

6 Which event happens FIRST?

   Ⓐ The friends gather for a feast.

   Ⓑ Cat comes to help the others pick the beet.

   Ⓒ The beet finally comes out of the ground.

   Ⓓ Potter comes over the hill.

7 Which title would make the best new name for this poem?

- Ⓐ "The Stubborn Cat"
- Ⓑ "The Farmer and His Friends Pick a Beet"
- Ⓒ "Large Vegetables"
- Ⓓ "Hunger on the Farm"

8 What is the result of the Cat joining the work?

- Ⓐ The Dog and the Sheep work harder.
- Ⓑ The beet grows toward the sun.
- Ⓒ The beet comes out of the ground.
- Ⓓ Peggy plants more beet seeds.

9 The Farmer thanks his friends for their persistence. What word has the same meaning as *persistence*?

- Ⓐ cleverness
- Ⓑ examination
- Ⓒ hope
- Ⓓ endurance

10 At the end of the story, the Farmer is

- Ⓐ looking for his dog.
- Ⓑ thankful.
- Ⓒ bad at farming.
- Ⓓ unlucky.

DIRECTIONS

Read this article by someone who enjoys writing. Then answer questions 1 through 10.

A Good Book

by Shakira Halsey

When I was in the fourth grade, my teacher had a great idea. She brought in colorful pieces of wallpaper and construction paper. She asked each of us to choose one piece of wallpaper and one piece of construction paper. She told us that we were going to make books to write in. She showed us how to fold the wallpaper to make a cover. We pasted the construction paper inside it. When we finished, we had strong, nice-looking covers. To make the inside pages, we folded pieces of plain white paper. We stapled the cover and the white paper together along the fold. Each of us had made our own book!

Every Wednesday afternoon was called Writing Wednesday. We took out our books and wrote whatever we wanted in them. We could even draw illustrations to decorate what we wrote. Some people liked to keep a diary or journal in their book. Some wrote stories and poems. I remember one story I wrote. It was about sitting on the clouds outside a castle in the sky. Sometimes I just wrote about a family picnic or what I had done at recess. Our writing didn't get graded. The teacher just checked to make sure that we wrote in our books. The next year, we didn't have Writing Wednesdays anymore. Some of my friends and I realized that we missed writing. We decided to get diaries and start writing on our own.

You wouldn't think that such a simple thing would matter, but it did. I became much more comfortable with the idea of writing. No matter what I had to write, I felt confident that I could do it. That really helped me when I was older. In middle school and high school, I often was assigned a project that involved writing. I wrote papers about the books I read. I wrote my opinion on different topics. I think that if you write a lot when you are young, you will be a better writer when you are older. You might even have fun writing.

I kept the book that I made in fourth grade and the diaries that I wrote later. Every so often I look at them and I read about something that I had forgotten. Sometimes I see what once worried me or what music I used to like, and I laugh. Go ahead, make a diary or a book that you can write in every once in a while. Even if you find writing hard now, keep the things that you write so that you can recollect who you used to be. Who knows? You may become a great author someday!

1 When the author made her book as a child, what did she do FIRST?

- (A) She stapled the paper along the fold line.
- (B) She folded the paper in half.
- (C) She picked a piece of wallpaper.
- (D) She wrote in the book.

2 What was one effect of Writing Wednesdays?

- (A) Wednesday afternoons were used for math lessons.
- (B) The author grew more confident.
- (C) The class grew tired of writing.
- (D) Everyone in the class wrote poetry.

3 What is the main idea of this story?

- (A) You should pick a day every week to write.
- (B) The more you write, the better a writer you will be.
- (C) Writing should only be done on Wednesdays.
- (D) Writing is not useful.

4 A diary will help you recollect who you used to be. What does *recollect* mean?

- (A) erase
- (B) recall
- (C) believe
- (D) forget

5 What is likely to happen if you write every day?

- (A) You will become a better writer.
- (B) Your writing will get worse.
- (C) You will have to write down everything that happens to you.
- (D) You will be able to illustrate your work.

6 What is a material that the children used to make their covers?

   Ⓐ twine

   Ⓑ spiral notebooks

   Ⓒ construction paper

   Ⓓ yarn

7 The author's high school projects often involved writing. What does *involve* mean?

   Ⓐ copy

   Ⓑ include

   Ⓒ erase

   Ⓓ admire

8 What was one reason that the author liked Writing Wednesdays?

   Ⓐ She enjoyed reading.

   Ⓑ She liked to write about her dog.

   Ⓒ She was able to write whatever she wanted.

   Ⓓ She never got to write.

9 What name would make the best title for this article?

   Ⓐ "Why Wednesday is a Good Day to Write"

   Ⓑ "How a Book is Published"

   Ⓒ "What I Wrote in High School"

   Ⓓ "Practice Your Writing to Become a Better Writer"

10 What caused the author to keep a diary?

   Ⓐ She missed Writing Wednesdays.

   Ⓑ She wanted a book with a key.

   Ⓒ She wanted to remember everything she did.

   Ⓓ Her friends all had them.

DIRECTIONS

Read this story about one of our senses.
Then answer questions 1 through 10.

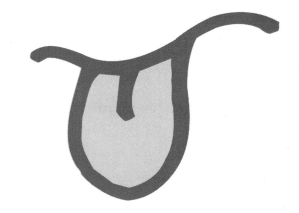

Good Taste
by Jasmine Thomas

In your head, you have eyes that let you see, ears that let you hear, a nose that lets you smell, and to let you taste—the tongue. The tongue is a muscle. It can wiggle, bend, twist, and turn. This ability to move helps the tongue change shape as you talk. When it comes to the job of sensing taste, however, it is the surface of the tongue that is important.

Try this simple experiment: First, make different mixtures. Make one mixture that is sweet by mixing water with sugar. Make a mixture that is salty by mixing water with salt. Make a mixture that is bitter by mixing water and tonic, and make a mixture that is sour by mixing water and lemon juice. Second, stick out your tongue in order to dry it. Then dip a cotton swab in one of the mixtures. Touch the swab to each part of your tongue. Where is the swab touching when you taste the sour lemon juice? Where is it when you taste the salty water? You will find that each part of your tongue can sense different tastes. The tip of your tongue, for example, senses sweetness.

How does your tongue sense taste? Look at the surface of your tongue. If you take a close look, you will find that this top part has many little bumps called **papillae**. Each papilla contains **taste buds** that do the job of tasting. When you eat an orange, your mouth waters. When your mouth waters, it is making **saliva.** The saliva breaks down the orange into tiny parts as you chew. When you eat an orange, the taste buds in the salty, sweet, bitter, and sour areas on your tongue sense the chemicals that make up the orange. You also have special taste buds that sense heat and cold. Each taste bud on the tongue senses something different. They all work together so you can taste and feel the orange.

Taste is an important sense to almost every living being. Taste helps us tell foods that are safe to eat from those that are not. For example, if you bit into a rotten apple, you would know right away that you had better not eat it! Taste can also protect animals and plants from being eaten. For example, some toads give off a bitter liquid that covers their skin. This bitter liquid is not edible. It tastes so bad that an animal that tries to eat one of the toads takes a single lick and then avoids all toads for the rest of its life.

Our sense of taste helps people and animals eat. Perhaps, if worms tasted like sweet, juicy strawberries, we would be making worm pies, wormcicles, or even worms dipped in chocolate! 🍎

Good Taste 51

1 Which step should you do FIRST in the tongue experiment?

(A) Dip cotton swabs in different mixtures.

(B) Stick your tongue out to dry it.

(C) Touch a cotton swab to different parts of your tongue.

(D) Prepare four different mixtures to taste.

2 "Look at the surface of your tongue." What is the *surface*?

(A) the top part

(B) the salty area

(C) the little bumps

(D) the muscle

3 What part of the tongue contains the taste buds?

(A) the paprika

(B) the mixtures

(C) the papillae

(D) the chemicals

4 Based on what you have read, you might say that the tongue

(A) is very limited in what it can do.

(B) is a mystery to modern science.

(C) has an important job in keeping people alive.

(D) is missing in most animals.

5 What causes you to sense a sweet taste?

 (A) Tiny parts of a sweet food touch the tip of your tongue.

 (B) Tiny parts of a sweet food touch the sides of your tongue.

 (C) Tiny parts of a sweet food touch the back of your tongue.

 (D) Your sweet tooth bites into a sweet food.

6 What is another good title for this selection?

 (A) "Why Toads are Bitter"

 (B) "The Tongue Senses Taste"

 (C) "How to Do an Interesting Experiment"

 (D) "Sweeter is Better"

7 Some toads give off a bitter liquid that is not edible. It tastes so bad that an animal that tries to eat one of the toads takes a single lick and then avoids all toads for the rest of its life. What is the meaning of *edible*?

 (A) able to be eaten

 (B) hot and spicy

 (C) bad tasting

 (D) too sweet

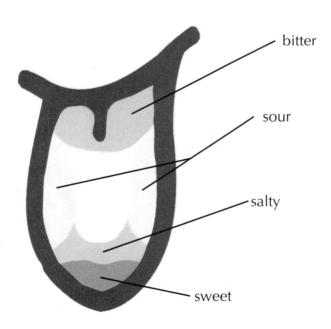

READING COMPREHENSION: SELECTION 9

8. Which of the following events happens FIRST?

  (A) Taste buds sense cold, heat, and pressure.

  (B) Taste buds work together to sense the taste and feel of food.

  (C) The mouth begins to water.

  (D) Chewing breaks down the food into tiny parts.

9. What tastes are sensed by the different parts of the tongue?

  (A) bitter, sweet, sour, and spicy

  (B) strong, weak, and fruity

  (C) crunchy, slimy, sour, and salty

  (D) bitter, sweet, sour, and salty

10. What is the main idea of this selection?

  (A) Our senses are important to staying alive.

  (B) Many animals will avoid eating toads.

  (C) The tongue allows animals and people to sense taste.

  (D) Don't gobble your food.

DIRECTIONS

Read this story that teaches a lesson about how people should behave. Then answer questions 1 through 10.

The Rock in the Road
retold by Alan Brenner

A long time ago, there lived a queen who ruled her people with great kindness. Queen Nadine loved every person and animal who called her kingdom home. Rulers all over the world heard about her benevolence and good heart. People often saw her chatting with shopkeepers, making sure the children were doing well in school, and visiting the sick. When a problem arose, the good people of Capabianca asked Queen Nadine for her wise advice. The queen was so helpful that people all over the world traveled to Capabianca to meet her.

One afternoon, Queen Nadine looked out her window and viewed the scenery. She looked at the town square. Its streets sparkled with the energy of shoppers, children, and animals. She wanted her people to care for each other as much as she cared for them. Someday she might want to leave her kingdom to visit faraway places. She wanted to be sure that the good people of Capabianca would help each other while she was gone. After some thinking, Queen Nadine decided to test her people. How else would she know if the citizens of Capabianca were thoughtful and caring?

As night fell over the kingdom, the queen went down to the main road that led to the town square. She pushed a large rock into the middle of the road and hid behind a tree to watch.

In the morning, a farmer in a wagon loaded with vegetables came down the road. When he saw the rock blocking the road, he began to grumble. "Who could be so lazy as to leave this stone right in the middle of the road? It could have damaged my new wagon," he cried. With a huff of disgust and a scowl on his face, the farmer drove his wagon around the rock and went on his way.

Later, two knights came trotting down the road on their horses. One knight boasted about how brave and skillful he was. The other knight claimed that he could win any competition. When they saw the rock in the road, they rolled their eyes. "How could someone be stupid enough to leave a rock in the middle of the road? It is quite dangerous," one knight exclaimed to the other. "My horse might have been hurt if she had tripped over it!" The two men complained and rode around the stone.

All day long, Queen Nadine watched people walk around the stone complaining. No one even tried to move the stone.

As the day came to a close, Queen Nadine grew sadder. She realized that her people did not care enough about others to move the rock. Instead of solving the problem, they just complained about how it might have hurt them.

At last, a young woman came along. She was returning from a long day working at the mill. Rubbing her eyes and yawning, the young woman saw the rock in the road. "Someone might fall over this stone in the dark and get hurt," she said aloud. "I better move it out of the way."

The young woman tugged and pushed with all her strength and finally managed to move the stone to the side of the road. Then she saw a box on the ground where the stone had been. On the box was written, "This box belongs to the one who moves the stone." The young woman was curious. She wondered what could be inside. Opening the box, she found that it was filled with gold coins! She ran home happily to her family and showed them her discovery.

When others heard of the young woman's good fortune, they wished they had earned the riches. "My friends," Queen Nadine said, "we are always rewarded when we help others. How can our kingdom succeed if we do not watch out for each other?"

1. Why does Queen Nadine put the rock in the road?

   (A) She wants to test her people to see if they will care for each other.

   (B) She wants to damage the farmer's new wagon.

   (C) She wants to give her money away.

   (D) She wants to take time off from helping others.

2. What is the best title for this story?

   (A) "Queen Nadine's Test"

   (B) "Why We Have Roads"

   (C) "Life in Capabianca"

   (D) "The Boastful Knights"

3. The young woman in the story is

   (A) selfish.

   (B) well educated.

   (C) clear.

   (D) thoughtful.

4. The story says that rulers all over the world heard of the queen's benevolence. What is *benevolence*?

   (A) goodness

   (B) trickiness

   (C) coldness

   (D) knowledge of science

The Rock in the Road 57

5 What is the farmer carrying in his wagon?

(A) grain

(B) vegetables

(C) apples

(D) people

6 Which of the following events happens FIRST?

(A) Two knights walk down the road.

(B) A young woman moves the rock.

(C) The queen hides behind a tree.

(D) The queen puts the rock in the road.

7 What does Queen Nadine mean when she says, "We are always rewarded when we help others"?

(A) When we help others, we will always find gold.

(B) When we help others, our queen will always stay.

(C) When we help others, it always helps the whole community.

(D) When we help others, we will get good jobs.

8   What is the theme of the story?

    (A) If you complain, you will always get what you want.

    (B) Take care of yourself first.

    (C) Caring for others is important, even if it takes a lot of work.

    (D) Everyone will seek your advice.

9   The story says that the young woman was curious about the box. What does *curious* mean?

    (A) wondering

    (B) foolish

    (C) insulting

    (D) generous

10   What happens AFTER the young woman returns home with the gold coins?

    (A) The queen rewards her with more riches.

    (B) People wish they had earned the gold coins.

    (C) The young woman gives her coins away.

    (D) The young woman puts the rock back in the middle of the road.

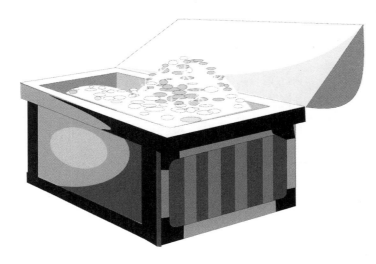

The Rock in the Road   **59**

Tips
for Multiple-Choice Questions

When you answer multiple-choice questions, remember these tips:

📖 Before looking at the answers, decide what you think the answer is. Then see if your answer is among the choices.

📖 Rule out obviously wrong answers first. Then choose, from the answers that are left, the one that seems most likely.

📖 Find out if extra points are taken off for wrong answers. If not, take your best guess. You will have some chance of choosing the right answer.

📖 Remember that on multiple-choice tests, you are supposed to choose the BEST answer to the question. If one answer is partly right, look for another that is completely right.

📖 If you do not know the answer to a question, go on to the other questions and come back later to the one you cannot answer. Answering the other questions might provide a clue or help to jog your memory.

📖 If a multiple-choice question is a sentence completion or fill-in-the-blank type, check your answer by reading the whole sentence, with the answer in it, silently to yourself. (Example: Yammer made a bedroom in _____. [the bookcase])

📖 Watch out for words in directions like *not* or *except*. (Example: Which of the following sentences is *not* true?)

📖 Also pay attention to any words or phrases in directions or answers that tell how many, such as *all, many, most, some, none,* or *a few*. (Example: *Some* wild animals need help from people.)

TIPS